The Thin Book Of®

Appreciative Inquiry

By Sue Annis Hammond

2nd edition

*W*hat You Are Going To Read

*t*his book is an invitation to begin your journey to learn about Appreciative Inquiry. Appreciative Inquiry is an exciting philosophy for change. The major assumption of Appreciative Inquiry is that in every organization something works and change can be managed through the identification of what works, and the analysis of how to do more of what works. This work is a "translation" of what I have learned from David Cooperrider of Case Western Reserve University and his many associates and fellow explorers.

Wonderful, thick, rich writing on Appreciative Inquiry is now available in many forms. But where do you begin? I wrote this book because I'm overwhelmed by the challenge of keeping up with professional development. My colleagues and clients tell me they are too. How do we learn enough about new theories to decide which ones we will commit to master?

For: RBH

AUTHOR:
Sue Annis Hammond

DESIGNER:
Alisann Marshall

ISBN 0-9665373-1-9
2nd edition
November 1998

*b*ecause of my interest in Appreciative Inquiry, I was getting calls for help from other professionals. Did I have anything like a summary I could send them? I sent out what I had but I knew it didn't do justice to this wonderful philosophy. So after three such calls one morning, I began the Thin Book. The title "Thin" is meant to describe what this contains as well as what it does not contain. The intent was and is to give you enough to decide whether you want to make the larger commitment necessary to internalize this work.

David Cooperrider resisted creating a "manual" for Appreciative Inquiry because he worried it would turn into another technique or fad of the month. I share his concerns, yet, as a change management consultant, I find that Appreciative Inquiry, like a lot of good ideas, is being shared in fragmented ways. I have attempted to pull enough pieces together to allow you to glimpse the beautiful picture and to inspire you to read the underlying theory. The resource section contains many of the published references.

The Thin Book is for those who want to find out what it is about before they invest the time to really learn it! Additionally, there are now many resources on the internet. Visit the AI Commons at: http://appreciativeinquirity.case.edu.

A key principle of Appreciative Inquiry is that it is a generative process. That means it is a moving target and is created and constantly re-created by the people who use it. Unlike a cookbook approach to change, Appreciative Inquiry is a thought process. Every participant makes a contribution, so I encourage you to read, dream, and experience. Let me know how it goes.

SUE ANNIS HAMMOND

THIN BOOK PUBLISHING CO.

70 SW CENTURY DRIVE

STE. 100-446

BEND, OR 97702

WWW.THINBOOK.COM

5.

What is Appreciative Inquiry?

WHAT PROBLEMS ARE YOU HAVING?
WHAT IS WORKING AROUND HERE?

*t*hese two questions underline the difference between traditional Change Management theory and Appreciative Inquiry. The traditional approach to change is to look for the problem, do a diagnosis, and find a solution. The primary focus is on what is wrong or broken; since we look for problems, we find them. By paying attention to problems, we emphasize and amplify them. This approach is consistent with a historical attitude in American Business that sees human systems as machines and parts (people) as interchangeable. We believe we can fix anything and there is a right answer or solution to any organizational problem or challenge.

In the mid-eighties, David Cooperrider and his associates at Case Western Reserve University, challenged this approach and introduced the term *Appreciative Inquiry*. David's artist wife Nancy brought the "appreciative eye" perspective to David's attention. The idea of the appreciative eye assumes that in every piece of art there is beauty. Art is a beautiful idea translated into a concrete form[1]. Cooperrider applied the notion to business: to the appre-

6 .

ciative eye, organizations are expressions of beauty and spirit. Furthermore, organizations are viewed as organic, which means that all parts are defined by the whole; thus, you cannot take an organization apart to study pieces.

Appreciative Inquiry suggests that we look for what works in an organization. The tangible result of the inquiry process is a series of statements that describe where the organization wants to be, based on the high moments of where they have been. Because the statements are grounded in real experience and history, people know how to repeat their success.

It is this energy that distinguishes the generative process that results from Appreciative Inquiry.

Through a workshop format, the participants stir up memories of energizing moments of success creating a new energy that is positive and synergistic. Participants walk away with a sense of commitment, confidence and affirmation that they have been successful. They also know clearly how to make more moments of success. It is this energy that distinguishes the generative process that results from Appreciative Inquiry. There is no end,

7 .

because it is a living process. Because the statements generated by the participants are grounded in real experience and history, people know how to repeat their success.

*t*he idea, then, is to approach organizations with an appreciative eye. A senior manager at GTE described Appreciative Inquiry and cautioned the group that he wasn't advocating mindless happy talk. But he asked them, when you get a survey that says 94% of your customer are happy, what do you automatically do? You probably interview the unhappy 6%, instead of asking the 94% what we did to make them happy.[2]

At this point, the cynic in all of us kicks in. Isn't this a rather simplistic way to face an organization's incredible challenges? Isn't this a naive approach? You may hear that dismissive voice. If so, I challenge you to suspend cynicism and experience Appreciative Inquiry. There is no other way to discover how it works and, indeed, how practical it is, until you do it. You do not have to have a major change program in order to experiment. You can

start with something as simple as asking a question at
the end of a meeting:

WHAT DID WE, AS A GROUP, DO WELL IN THIS MEETING?

*Y*ou will get a stunned silence. Then people will
begin to throw out some very carefully worded
responses. Depending on your position and
title, they will try to figure out the politically
correct response. Responses will quickly turn into a discussion about what didn't work. We are very good at
talking about what doesn't work. We have all had years
of practice in the art of problem-solving and in being
exhorted to be part of the solution. It is my opinion, that
we have little practice looking for what works and finding ways to do more of that. It never occurs to us that
we can "fix" an organization or even our society by doing
more of what works. We are obsessed with learning
from our mistakes. But, why not allow our successes to
multiply.enough to crowd out the unsuccessful? Why
not follow-up with our happy customers and ask why
we made them happy?

We are very good at talking about what doesn't work.

9.

An Example

*M*any different cultures now meet regularly in the workplace. In the seventies this created a demand for sexual harassment prevention training, which evolved into diversity training. The objective is to improve human relationships in the workplace while recognizing that individuals from diverse cultures have different ways of interpreting behavior. One of the more common methods used in sexual harassment prevention training focused on learning checklists of what not to do. I can still recall conducting EEO training that was intended to make participants aware of all the practices that were illegal.

A recent Wall Street Journal[3] article reported on such training of Japanese managers about to be sent to the US. Many articles and books in the management press have documented the wide differences between the Japanese and US corporate cultures. In preparation for their move to the US, the managers were given checklists of taboo behaviors such as reading pornographic magazines at work, staring at female colleagues' legs, and hugging employees. The Japanese managers were bewildered as to what they could do. One can almost envision them reviewing a little card with a list of don'ts on a daily basis.

If you've ever conducted or attended this type of training, you know it has potential to produce a rather negative environment. Also, there have been studies demonstrating an increase in the number of sexual harassment complaints in spite of, and perhaps as a result of, the training.[4] That makes sense, because participants are educated to be more aware of what not to do and are more sensitized to finding that behavior.

Share examples of what it feels like and looks like to be treated with dignity and respect.

W hen the appreciative approach is applied to the objective, participants are asked to share examples of what it feels like and looks like to be treated with dignity and respect. Participants determine the circumstances that make dignity and respect possible and articulate statements to express the common themes.

11 ·

Instead of taking away a list of don'ts and a policing mentality, participants leave inspired to re-create those circumstances in as many situations as possible.

The Obvious

*i*t seems so obvious doesn't it? Most change management consultants I know wonder why they did not think of this before. When I first learned about Appreciative Inquiry I spent a lot of time replaying many situations in which I had unwittingly infected groups with negative energy. I thought I was the neutral observer, helping my clients get "better." Instead, I left them more focused and eloquent on what was wrong. Asking appreciative questions, I still get the information I need but the difference is, the organization has the confirmed knowledge, confidence, and inspiration that they did well, and will continue to do well with a heightened awareness of what works. Not only do I have the gift of new eyes, but, hopefully others do too.

What Is The Role Of Assumptions In Change?

*i*n order to begin to understand Appreciative Inquiry, I believe you have to understand the role of assumptions in organizations. Organizations are made up of individuals who form groups to get work done. The groups behave according to the rules of group behavior.[5]   Assumptions are the set of beliefs shared by a group, that causes the group to think and act in certain ways.

For example, when someone in my family (group) sees a dog running in a park with no leash, he or she assumes the dog is dangerous and tries to stay out of the way. Why do members of my family assume that? We make that assumption based on the time I was bit by a dog without a leash. Naturally, I howled about it and told all the members of my family what happened. As a result, they began to behave differently around unleashed dogs. Over time, it became an unquestioned belief to this group that unleashed dogs were dangerous. As new members of the group (children) appear, the group teaches them to stay clear of all unleashed dogs because the dogs may bite.

> *Assumptions are the set of beliefs shared by a group, that causes the group to think and act in certain ways.*

13 ·

The downside
is that the
group may
fail to see
new data that
contradicts
their belief
and they may
miss an
opportunity to
improve their
effectiveness.

14 .

Within my family, the assumption that all unleashed dogs are dangerous has become a deeply held belief. It moved to an unconscious level so members of the group don't stop to think when they see an unleashed dog. Instead, they react in accordance with the belief that all unleashed dogs are dangerous. The longer the belief is in effect, the harder it is for the group to see any new information that contradicts the belief.

*t*he beauty of assumptions is they become a shorthand for the group. When faced with similar situations, a group just acts and doesn't re-evaluate each time. Groups have a large number of assumptions operating at an unconscious level. Shared assumptions allow the group to work efficiently because they don't have to constantly stop and determine what they believe and how they should act. The downside is that the group may fail to see new data that contradicts their belief and they may miss an opportunity to improve their effectiveness. This is why it is important to bring to the surface and evaluate group assumptions every so often to see if they are still valid.

ASSUMPTIONS ARE STATEMENTS OR
RULES THAT EXPLAIN WHAT A GROUP
GENERALLY BELIEVES.

ASSUMPTIONS EXPLAIN THE CONTEXT OF
THE GROUP'S CHOICES AND BEHAVIORS.

ASSUMPTIONS ARE USUALLY NOT VISIBLE
TO OR VERBALIZED BY
THE PARTICIPANTS/MEMBERS;
RATHER THEY DEVELOP AND EXIST.

ASSUMPTIONS MUST BE MADE VISIBLE
AND DISCUSSED BEFORE ANYONE CAN
BE SURE OF THE GROUP BELIEFS.[6]

15

You signal
you know the
rules by wear-
ing what is
expected of a
group member.

*t*o better understand the way assumptions work, let's look at an example everybody can relate to: dressing for success. In corporate America, dressing for success means wearing clothing that shows that you know the assumptions (rules) of the group. For a long time, the classic symbol or shorthand to show you knew the rules, was to wear a tailored suit. For years, IBM told new employees that dark blue suits and white shirts were required to symbolize the IBM way of doing business. Other companies had and still have their version of a dress code. Wearing the uniform was a shorthand symbol representing your connection to the organization. If you don't know the rules, you are not going to be considered for membership in the group. You signal you know the rules by wearing what is expected of a group member.

Recently the assumption that one had to wear a tailored suit to be a productive employee has been questioned by the widespread acceptance of "business casual". Look around you on Fridays in business class on airplanes and in many organizations. People wear Dockers and Rockports and apparently work still gets done.

I watched a client organization go through the transition to business casual, first on Fridays only, then summer only, then all year-round. At the beginning, people were upset at the organization for changing the dress code. They complained that the company was making them buy new clothes. I thought the complaints actually expressed fear that they would not know what to wear to fit in, or in some cases, how to express their status through business casual.

After Labor Day, when they were supposed to go back to "regular" clothes, employees were angry because they had learned to like the more casual approach. They also told me that the change had created a more relaxed attitude during the summer months, which made them feel more productive. The assumption that employees had to wear suits, ties, and other professional dress in order to be productive, respected employees was questioned

17

through actual experience. Men and women found it easier to think without a tie or pantyhose. The experience proved to them, that the uniform made no difference, and they now dress in business casual all year.

Uneasiness may stem from the fear of doing something wrong, which signals you don't belong to the group.

Watching a long-held assumption be questioned and replaced tends to inspire people to question other long-held assumptions. In my opinion, this is the first step necessary for any organizational change. One of the reasons organizational change is so hard is that it produces an uneasy feeling. One reason for the uneasiness is a fear of doing something wrong, which signals that you don't belong to the group.

In another client organization, one department manager declared that because they did not have direct client contact, they would begin business casual dress. Members of the department showed up on Monday in

18 ·

business casual. By the end of the week, most were back in the traditional uniform. When questioned why, they reported that they "felt funny in business casual." The larger group, the organization, was still in suits and the department members interacted with them in hallways and at the elevator. Even though this group did not have direct customer contact, they did have constant contact with other members of the organization. In business casual, they did not look like the other members of the organization and they were very uncomfortable. To feel like members of the group, they went back to wearing what other members of the group wore.[7]

The shared set of assumptions of a group is a powerful force. One needs to understand what the assumptions are, in order to predict how the group will act. To understand Appreciative Inquiry, one must understand the assumptions.

19.

Assumptions of Appreciative Inquiry

1. In every society, organization, or group, something works.

2. What we focus on becomes our reality.

3. Reality is created in the moment, and there are multiple realities.

4. The act of asking questions of an organization or group influences the group in some way.

5. PEOPLE HAVE MORE CONFIDENCE AND COMFORT TO JOURNEY TO THE FUTURE (THE UNKNOWN) WHEN THEY CARRY FORWARD PARTS OF THE PAST (THE KNOWN).

6. IF WE CARRY PARTS OF THE PAST FORWARD, THEY SHOULD BE WHAT IS BEST ABOUT THE PAST.

7. IT IS IMPORTANT TO VALUE DIFFERENCES.

8. THE LANGUAGE WE USE CREATES OUR REALITY.

*T*hey Look Good...

*t*his set of assumptions may look reasonable to you. After all, they sound politically correct. The application of the assumptions may be a different matter. If you react emotionally or defensively to any of the assumptions, it might represent one that counters an assumption you believe.

For example, if you are a consultant and accept assumption 4, you have to throw out your identity as a neutral observer. Your very presence affects the group in some way. This assumption is fundamentally different from the traditional research model which assumes that we can enter and leave a group as neutral (scientific) observers.

*t*he most common question I hear from colleagues trying Appreciative Inquiry demonstrates to me why it is important to understand all of the assumptions. For example, they start out with the question "what did we do well in this meeting?"

22 ·

Because they are still in the problem-solving model, they apply the answers to the group's deficits. How can we do better as a result of what we didn't do well, is the underlying assumption for the problem-solving model.

Contrast the appreciative mindset: We know that we have performed well at something (assumption 1) and need to explore how that happened and how to do more. Doing more of what works is the driver for Appreciative Inquiry as opposed to doing less of something we do not do well in the problem-solving model. In my experience, you cannot use Appreciative Inquiry as a questioning technique within the problem-solving model and achieve the desired result. For Appreciative Inquiry to work its magic, you have to believe and internalize the assumptions. That comes with study and practice.

The model on the following page, developed by Cooperrider and Srivastva[8] contrasts problem-solving with Appreciative Inquiry.

APPRECIATIVE INQUIRY FOCUS: Doing more of what works.

PROBLEM-SOLVING FOCUS: Doing less of something we do not do well.

23 .

PROBLEM SOLVING	APPRECIATIVE INQUIRY
"Felt Need" *Identification of Problem*	*Appreciating and Valuing* *The Best of "What Is"*
	↓
Analysis of Causes	*Envisioning "What Might Be"*
	↓
Analysis of Possible Solutions	*Dialoguing "What Should Be"*
	↓
Action Planning *(Treatment)*	*Innovating "What Will Be"*
BASIC ASSUMPTION: **AN ORGANIZATION IS A** **PROBLEM TO BE SOLVED**	**BASIC ASSUMPTION:** **AN ORGANIZATION IS A MYSTERY** **TO BE EMBRACED**

Adapted from Cooperrider and Srivastva (1987) "Appreciative Inquiry Into Organizational Life" in *Research in Organizational Change and Development.* Pasmore and Woodman (eds) Vol 1, JAI Press

*a*nother fundamental difference of Appreciative Inquiry is the belief that the language we use creates our reality (assumption 8). All words have definitions but some words have emotional meanings as well. There are neutral words such as: *the, at, on.* Other words such as, *dysfunctional, co-dependent, stress, addiction, depressed, and burned out,* are part of a vocabulary Ken Gergen[9] terms the "language of deficit." Many of the words have been used in a clinical setting only in the past twenty years but, are now also used in organizations. The emotional meaning in the words we use affects our thinking.

*t*o understand how word choice can influence large bodies, consider President Jimmy Carter's focus on the "malaise in the country" just before his bid for re-election. It disturbed people to hear the leader of our country *say* that we had big problems, even if we *thought* we did. Ronald Reagan's optimism and insistence that we were great and glorious might have been the primary reason for Reagan's election, Carter's negative message his downfall. The nation is a big group, and the group rejected the leader who spoke of illness. Carter apparently broke with our national assumption that our leaders should only refer to other groups (nations) as ill. Curiously, the group may reject the negative messenger, but internalize the message. If an organization keeps hearing how ill it is and how much it has to fix itself, members will behave as if the organization were ill.

What we focus on becomes our reality. If we focus on what is wrong or what is missing, we tend to see everything through that filter or frame.

*I*f we accept Assumption 2, then what we focus on becomes our reality. If we focus on what is wrong or what is missing, we tend to see everything through that filter or frame. The filter or frame is our unconscious set of assumptions. We tend not to be aware of our frame, and we fail to notice that we disregard information that doesn't fit our reality. An example of the filter phenomenon is the Pygmalion effect or the halo effect. Research proved that students designated as

26 ·

high IQ were perceived differently by teachers. What might have been viewed as disruptive behavior in a lower IQ class , was viewed as positive or creative behavior in the high IQ class. In a way, the high IQ students could do no wrong and the low IQ students could not do much right.

A similar thing can happen in organizations. We teach managers to be aware of the halo effect in performance reviews. When a person rated as high-performing is constantly viewed through the "halo" filter, what would be perceived as low performance in another person is refracted through the high-performing filter and viewed as more high performance. In order to see data that conflict with our assumptions, we have to break outside of our filter or frame. Chris Argyris calls the frame, theories in use, Edgar Schein and Peter Senge call it a mental model. All point out that the frame can inhibit learning because data that does not fit the frame is inconceivable and is often undiscussable. [10]

BREAKING THROUGH THE FRAME

*f*rames can also be negative. An interesting example of breaking the frame of an extremely negative situation through Appreciative Inquiry is the case of a hotel called Medic Inn. Frank Barrett and David Cooperrider[11] describe a group locked in a frame of distrust and backbiting negativism. Barrett and Cooperrider quickly realized that to follow the traditional problem-solving approach would only further educate the group on their problems and unleash huge amounts of anxiety and defensiveness. Instead, they focus the group on a metaphor; a journey, literally taking the group on a journey to another city to see a top-rated hotel with an appreciative eye. The journey catches the group's attention because some of the members had never traveled on an airplane (this case took place in the seventies) nor stayed overnight in a four-star hotel.

The group learns enough of the basics of Appreciative Inquiry to conduct interviews with the staff at the award winning hotel. The interviews focused in finding out what made this property an award-winning enterprise.

28.

They shared their data with the hotel employees in the spirit of a gift. In the process of looking for and sharing what worked in another organization, the "dysfunctional" group realized that they, too, could work in similar ways and have similar results. They began to re-view their history in a new way, and this time found some things that worked. Barrett and Cooperrider report that the group's negative frame was broken through the journey. The group began to work together in a new ways, leading to their success some years later at becoming a top rated hotel. The metaphorical approach is similar to finding best practices and using benchmarking studies to generate new ideas across organizations.

● NEWER, STRONGER INTERESTS

*i*n the Medic Inn case the problem-solving frame would normally focus on fixing the relationships. Cooperrider and Barrett, like many others were inspired by Jung's[12] conclusion that problems are rarely solved on their own. To paraphrase Jung, an

29 ·

important problem is rarely solved, instead it is out-grown, as a newer, stronger interest comes along to crowd out the problem. When a newer and stronger urge or life force appears on the horizon, people adjust to grow towards it, much like a plant grows toward light. Creating a newer, stronger life urge is often the rationale behind creating organizational visions. Visualization theory has been around for a long time but may be most commonly known from athletics.

LESSONS FROM ATHLETICS

*a*ppreciative Inquiry also integrates something fascinating that we know from brain research: the brain does not hear the "not." When I say "Don't think of elephants," your brain only hears "Think of elephants." The most common application of this research is in athletics.

Cooperrider tells the story about a fellow golfer (who knows the research) tells David just before he hits the ball, "Don't hit it in the woods ". His brain hears, "Hit it in the woods". Contrast that with the more common approach of coaching an athlete to "see" the perfect performance. A coach would have David visualize hitting the ball straight down the middle, resulting in an improved golf game.

The tangible result of Appreciative Inquiry is a series of positive statements phrased as if they were already happening. Because they are amplifications of what has already happened, they are easily visualized. Organizational members grow toward the statements by doing more of what they have already done. Doing more of what works crowds out the insoluble problems. The next section will lead you through an example.

EXAMPLE
Instead of telling the golfer "Don't hit the ball into the woods", visualize the perfect performace and say "hit it straight down the middle"

31 ·

How To Do It
BEGIN WITH THE TOPIC

If what we focus on is magnified by our attention, we want to be sure we are magnifying something worthy.

Choosing your topic is the most critical step in the Appreciative Inquiry process. Because what we study becomes our reality (assumption 2) we want to be sure to study the right topic. In a large-scale systems change, choosing topics will probably take about two days. Those responsible for the topic choice should understand the seriousness of this step. You will not be able to take a topic off the organization's agenda once you begin to inquire about it. If what we focus on is magnified by our attention, we want to be sure we are magnifying something worthy. And we do not want to take on too much: even in a large scale effort, topic choice should be limited to five subjects.

For purposes of a simple example, let's say a team wants to do team-building. Team-building is not much of a topic, because it isn't specific enough. Deeper exploration might reveal that this team wants to learn how to get more done in their team meetings. I begin with the assumption that this team has done something well in

the past, as a group. I want to help them identify what
that is, how it happened, and how to do more of it in
their meetings. In order to discover these things, we ask
some questions. A clear topic definition is very important, because out of it come the questions necessary to
find out what you want to know.

CREATE THE QUESTIONS TO EXPLORE THE TOPIC

Start thinking about what questions you might ask to find
out what works in a team/group. Since Appreciative
Inquiry is a generative process, you create the questions
to explore your topic. Listed on the following page are
some sample questions. At this point, you, the reader,
have to stop reading and experience this for yourself.
When a book tells me to stop and do, I usually keep
reading and skip the exercise. However, experience
shows that you have to experience Appreciative Inquiry
to get it. So please stop now and answer the following
example questions considering a team, group, or organization of which you are or were a member.

33 ·

*S*ample *Questions*

Describe a time when you feel the team/group performed really well. What were the circumstances during that time?

Describe a time when you were proud to be a member of the team/group. Why were you proud?

What do you value most about being a member of this team/group? Why?

The Inquiry/Interview

O nce you create the questions, you offer them to the group. I suggest participants pair up and ask each other the questions. In small groups, you may have a group inquiry in which the group stays together and each member takes a turn answering the questions. Other applications use a team of employees to interview the entire organization or include the questions in a climate survey or focus groups. I recommend pair interviews as the most effective tool for exploration.

The questioner should jot down brief notes. As you question your partner, you will probably find that you want to ask other questions, share your experiences, or otherwise actively participate in the conversation. This is the difference between inquiry and standard rules of interviewing. For those trained in interviewing techniques, one tries to be the neutral, unbiased recorder. In Appreciative Inquiry, you do not have to follow that rule because of assumption number 4 (by asking questions of an organization or group, we have influenced the group in some way). It is OK to converse with your partner in the excitement of the moment (and appreciative interviews are exciting)!

WHAT TO DO WITH THE INFORMATION GENERATED BY THE INQUIRY

You might ask each person to share the best story, or the most "quotable quote."

When the pairs finish the inquiry, there is a lot of information between pairs. The goal is to share that information with the larger group in order to uncover common themes of circumstances when the group performed well. We want to uncover these themes in order to know how to do more of what worked.

If the size of the group permits, have all members share the most exciting information they learned from their interviews. You might ask each person to share the best story, or the most "quotable quote." Sharing information to uncover themes is messy. There is no checklist to follow; you have to work the process. This makes some

36 ·

people very nervous. They initially regard the process as a waste of time, because they can't see what they are going to do with the unorganized mass of information. Transforming the information into an applicable form follows, but first, the themes have to surface. And this will happen if you see the process through: Sharing will reveal common threads of success.

AN EXAMPLE

In one group, the topic was to explore extraordinary customer service. The questions were these:

> *Describe an incident when you or someone you know went the extra mile to provide the customer what they really wanted when they wanted it.*

> *What made that possible?*

Story after story recounted incidents in which people were touched by a customer's need, and took the initiative to help. The common themes of the circumstances that made extraordinary customer service possible were these:

37 .

THE RESULT:

➤ *Extraordinary*
Service is
provided.

➤ *Customer is*
pleasantly
surprised.

➤ *Service*
Provider feels
useful.

➤ *Service*
provider is
energized by
experience.

38 ·

AN EXAMPLE

THE PROVIDER

- *identified an opportunity.*
- *took responsibility.*
- *had the authority.*
- *had the data available.*
- *had the expertise.*
- *anticipated or articulated a need.*
- *trusted that the company would back them up.*

The result: Extraordinary service was provided and the customer was pleasantly surprised. The service provider felt useful and energized by the experience.

By creating this list, we discover within this group, what circumstances made it possible to provide extraordinary customer service. How does the group transform this knowledge into actions that will allow the successful circumstances to be re-created? To do this, the group begins by talking and dreaming about what could be, based on what has already happened. During this time

the group also creates "Provocative Propositions."
Provocative Propositions describe an ideal state of
circumstances that will foster the climate that creates
the possibilities to do more of what works.

Provocative Propositions:

WHY DO WE NEED THEM?

The purpose of provocative propositions is to keep our
best at a conscious level. They are symbolic statements
because they have meaning well beyond words, reminding us of what is best about the organization and how
everyone can participate in creating more of the best.
Provocative propositions are derived from stories that
actually took place in an organization. This grounding in
history, tradition, and facts distinguishes Appreciative
Inquiry from other visioning methods in which dreams
serve as the primary basis for the vision.

39 .

Grounding in history, tradition, and facts distinguishes Appreciative Inquiry from other visioning methods in which dreams serve as the primary basis for the vision.

Because provocative propositions are reality-based, organizational members connect to them and are inspired to do more of what works. The purchasing group at a large oil company wrote the following provocative proposition on customer service:

> *To us, customer service means satisfying the internal customer. Purchasing is a service organization that must meet the requirements of all customers, whatever and however different they might be from one to another. We encourage open communication with our customers and specifically ask them how we are doing.*

In my opinion, this is a clear and attractive set of directions on who the purchasing group thinks is important and how they will show the customer they are service-oriented.[13]

How To Write A Provocative Proposition

i n the first example on customer service, the group listed themes that made extraordinary service possible. The group then talked about what it would be like, if they ended their workdays with the knowledge that they had really helped someone. Every mind in the group is needed to envision what could be done to make the extraordinary possible on a daily basis. Taking time to talk together ensures that all minds are engaged. The process reflects the steps on page 42.

As A Group:

1. Find examples of the best (from the interviews).

2. Determine what circumstances made the best possible (in detail).

3. Take the stories and envision what might be. Write an affirmative statement (a provocative proposition) that describes the idealized future as if it were already happening.

To write the proposition, apply "what if" to all the common themes. Then write affirmative present-tense statements incorporating the common themes.

SAMPLE PROPOSITIONS
FROM THE EXAMPLE

Our customers have a pleasant experience when they talk to us.

We anticipate their needs and have the information available when they call.

We work through the information in an uninterrupted sequence and they talk to only one person.

The information we need to answer their questions is available to us with a touch of the finger.

We devote time to learning more so we keep our expertise current.

We do our best and know that our decisions are appreciated by others.

We feel comfortable providing extraordinary service for our clients because we know that is why they choose us.

We continually learn as we work.

We feel the support of our other organizational members and are confident we all know extraordinary service is how we help people.

43 .

Our business provides an important service to our customers.

We are proud to be a part of this organization.

Review the notes you made on the exercise at the beginning of this section. What commonalties appear in the circumstances that created pride or great performance from the team? Write one or two provocative propositions.

44 .

To determine whether this is a provocative proposition, check it against this criteria:

1. Is it provocative? Does it stretch, challenge or innovate?
2. Is it grounded in examples?
3. Is it what we want? Will people defend it or get passionate about it?
4. Is it stated in affirmative, bold terms and in present tense (as if it were already happening)?

Only the group can answer these questions and work through the necessary changes. To another group the propositions on page 43 may seem awfully tame. Given the current state of the technology and management style of this particular organization, this set of propositions was a stretch, a challenge, and bold. It describes where they want to be, based on the high moments of where they have been. It was also a symbol reminding them of the energized moments they found through their inquiry.

One early reviewer of this Thin Book was struck by how ordinary the list of provocative propositions seemed. This person said the list looked like every other list of customer-service "vision" statements. Where was the power reportedly created by Appreciative Inquiry, she asked? I knew the power and drama because I had been there when the list was created. Therein lies the answer to her excellent question. The power occurs when the group becomes engaged and excited. The whole energy of the group shifts and everyone there knows it! A good facilitator assists the group in acknowledging the difference in atmosphere and attitude. Provocative propositions have drama and power because they remind the group of the high points they have experienced Her question also reminded me how important it was to not only experience Appreciative Inquiry to get it, but to also understand the why (or assumptions) of the process. In my experience if appreciative questions are used to fix problems, the group is in the problem-solving model. Appreciative Inquiry does not work as a technique within the problem-solving paradigm.

45 ·

The Transforming Nature Of Appreciative Inquiry

Creating Provocative Propositions is a key step of transformation. We take what we know and we talk about what could be. We stretch what we are to help us be more than what we have already been successful at. We envision a future that is a collage of the Bests. Because we have derived the future from reality, we know it can happen. We can see it, we know what it feels like, and we move to a collective, collaborative view of where we are going. You can't skip the step of engaging the entire group to write the propositions, because this is where the momentum occurs. Try to get the whole group or a representative sample in one place at one time to work through this process.[14] Through the conversation necessary to reach agreement on the provocative propositions, everyone leaves their stamp. The set of propositions is a living document which will change as new ideas and circumstances occur. But during the life of the proposition, the members of the organization know what to do and how to grow toward the stated ideal.

The idea behind the group creation of propositions is to move the individual will to *group will*. *Group will* creates the synergy that results in a group achieving more than the sum of the individuals. *Group will* occurs when the group shares a clear goal that all members believe will happen and accordingly behave to make happen. This occurs only if the entire group is a part of the process and thus takes time. I find that once people become excited about the process through the questions, they make the time to have the group discussion. They realize quickly that this is not another fad of the month.

A Cautionary Tale

*i*n one unfortunate experience attempting to use Appreciative Inquiry, the manager of a group began attacking his employees for their responses. We had stayed together as a group and had taken turns giving answers to questions about what kind of work each person found most exciting. It became clear that what they found exciting did not fit their current job

Appreciative Inquiry touches something important and positive and people respond.

47 .

They don't give politically correct answers, they give heartfelt answers because we ask soulful questions. This information should be treated with dignity and respect.

descriptions and the boss called them on it. This manager had a history of employee abuse, but I had mistakenly trusted his expressed intention to learn how to manage differently. [15]

What I think is important about this story is that it points out an essential fact of Appreciative Inquiry. When you ask people appreciative questions, you touch something very important to them. They don't give politically correct answers, they give heartfelt answers because we ask soulful questions. This information should be treated with dignity and respect. More superficial questions would have protected those participants.

WHAT IS THE BUSINESS VALUE
OF THIS ENERGY?

*l*inking Appreciative Inquiry to measurable results in a business setting is one of the first questions I hear from managers. That is a fair question although the underlying assumption to that question, is that human systems can be quantified. If done well, most change strategies will create quantifiable results. And since I have my own business, I know I have to make money to stay in business. The data missing is how people feel while they are making enough money to stay in business. I have referred to the positive energy created by this work, several times in the text. In my experience, that positive energy is a result of people knowing how to create deeply satisfying results in an exciting way.

All of my work is based on the assumption that everyone wants to feel important and make a contribution. To me, this assumption represents my understanding of the human spirit. I choose to work with organizations because I see them as marvelous entities destined to do good. That is why when I choose a change model (and

49 .

there are many), I choose one that recognizes and honors the human spirit. The business value of Appreciative Inquiry is quantifiable results with a sense of joy.

Another business value of this process is that it will maintain the best of the organization. The danger of change models that start by throwing everything away is that the baby may be thrown out with the bath water. I find that people are generally proud to belong to their organization. That source of pride is often the most untapped natural resource within the organization. People want the organization to do purposeful work and they want to be a recognized part of it. Finding out why people are proud and excited to be there is an enormously wonderful process. And once you experience it, you also see how practical and applicable this is. Some change models or consultants create feel-good entertainment but the effect leaves with the speaker. This process engages all members of the organization in a positive and productive manner and manages the continuity of the organization.[16]

A QUANTIFIABLE EXAMPLE

*t*he retail locations of a large car repair organization used Appreciative Inquiry to improve customer satisfaction. Their challenge was to figure out how to get commitment to their vision from all employees. They did it by training one or two representative employees per location to gather stories of high quality service experiences. The representatives gathered in one location and shared their stories. They dialogued about what could be and created provocative propositions. The representatives returned to their locations to get the input of the other employees on what had been written.

Eventually, the feedback was rolled up to create propositions that everyone had touched. Employees could relate and act in accordance with the propositions because they "lived them" at one time or another. A survey agency measured their customer satisfaction level as 89% of customers were 100% satisfied. Those are great numbers for the auto repair industry.

Propositions are reality based because they're derived from actual stories. Employees can relate and act in accordance with propositions because they've "lived them".

51 ·

Innovation and Action

*t*he next part of the process is to let it emerge spontaneously. Let action and innovation occur in the moment. Be creative about integrating the provocative propositions in the organization. Know that the process is just that — a process. It lives, and change will occur. There is no end, because it is generative. Unlike other methodologies that are recipes, the results are invented with experience. Remember assumption 3: Reality is created in the moment, so each experience will differ. I hope that this Thin Book gives you enough courage to experiment. I invite you to teach and share as you learn.

This is the end of the Thin Book. It may seem like there ought to be more —there is. The "more" is in your experience and further study. I again emphasize the generative nature of this process. It grows and develops as people practice it. The objective of this book is to share the basics and let you decide if this is a subject you wish to master. It is at this point in the book, I could spend pages expounding to you why I think you should consider mastering this body of work. But this is not the purpose of the book or the philosophy of Appreciative Inquiry. I think that the one key assumption of Appreciative Inquiry is to learn to value differences. If you have made it this far in the book, you have demonstrated that you want to learn about something different. Your choice to go forward or stop may be different from mine and staying true to Appreciative Inquqiry, I honor your choice. Thank you for taking the time to get here. Enjoy your journey and let me know how it goes.

With Appreciation,
Sue Annis Hammond
November, 1998

53 .

Footnotes

1 Hegel from Adams, p.517.

2 See T.White in Vital Speeches.

3 See Wall Street Journal 7/9/96.

4 From 1990-1993 the percentage of sexual harassment charges (compared to total charges) at the EEOC rose from 5.4% to 8.3 %. Also see Ellis and Sonnnenfeld.

5 See Mink for a good primer on group behavior.

6 See Argyris, Schon, Schein for the best explanations of assumptions.

7 Thanks to Al Stroud for this example.

8 In Research on Organizational Change and Development, 1987.

9 See Gergen.

10 See Resource section for works by Argyris, Schein and Senge

11 Barrett and Cooperrider (1990).

12 See Jung.

13 Thanks to John Roarty for this example.

14 See Mohrman and Weisbord for ideas on large group change.

15 This is also a great example of the difference between what someone says and how they act. He was not as they say, walking the talk.

16 See Srivastva and Fry for more on organizational continuity.

Thanks to my colleagues and friends who took
time to read my drafts
and provide feedback.
Special thanks to Alisann
Marshall, Dana Joseph and
Martha O'Brien for their
extraordinary support.
And this book never would have
happened without
David Cooperrider's generosity
and support.

Sample Questions

THE THREE CLASSIC QUESTIONS

*1. Think back through your career in this organization.
Locate a moment that was a high point, when you felt most
effective and engaged. Describe how you felt, and what
made the situation possible.*

*2. Without being humble, describe what you value most
about your self, your work, your organization.*

*3. Describe your three concrete wishes for the future of this
organization.*

ETHICS AND INTEGRITY

*1. Describe a person, organization or incident that you feel
is a great example of someone being fair. What were the circumstances that led to it? What were the consequences?*

*2. Think of a person whom you admire for his/her integrity.
Think of a specific incident, a time and place where you saw
this person demonstrate high integrity. Describe the circumstances and the consequences*

TEAMWORK

*Describe a time when you were a part of or observed an extra-
ordinary display of cooperation between diverse organizations or groups What made that cooperation possible?*

CUSTOMER SERVICE

Describe an incident when you or someone you know went the extra mile to deliver what the customer wanted when they wanted it. What made it possible?

VALUE ADDED

Describe a moment or example when you or someone you know was recognized by a "I could not have done this without you" letter, phone call, e-mail, public acknowledgment, etc.? What were the circumstances and how did people feel afterward?

SUPPLIER RELATIONSHIPS

If you could transform the supply-chain relationship any way you wish, what would it look like and what three things would you do?

TRUST

Describe a time when you were part of a team that had a high level of trust and respect among the members. How was trust and respect communicated? What made it possible to establish trust in that group?

Sample Questions

VALUING DIFFERENCES

Think back over your adult life and think of a person for whom you had a great deal of respect but didn't always agree with. When you disagreed with that person, how did you communicate that? What made it possible for you to maintain respect for that person?

THE CLASSIC QUESTIONS APPLIED TO YOUR PROFESSIONAL LIFE

1. Describe the most energizing moment, a real "high" from your professional life. What made it possible?

2. Without being humble, describe what you value most about your self, and your profession. If you are new to the profession, what attracted you to it?

3. Describe how you stay professionally affirmed, renewed, energized, enthusiastic, inspired?

4. Describe your three concrete wishes for the future of your profession.

Sue Annis Hammond is a Change Management Consultant with a unique combination of extensive consulting experience, academic training and entrepreneurial success. She has over thirty years of consulting experience including ten years of internal work, twenty years of external consulting and over ten years entrepreneurial experience in founding and running a business (www.thinbook.com). Sue completed a Master's of Organizational Development at Bowling Green Graduate School of Business, where she was the 1991 Minninger Foundation Fellow. She also holds a BA and MA in English.

Sue is also the co-author of **The Thin Book of Naming Elephants: How to Surface Undiscussables for Greater Organizational Success.** *Because of the original thin book's success and requests from customers for more thin books, Sue founded Thin Book Publishing Co. This company is devoted to publishing "just in time" cutting-edge knowledge to organizational clients.*

You can reach Sue at: Sue@thinbook.com.

Resources

Adams, Hazard. (ed.) *Critical Theory Since Plato.* Harcourt, Brace Jovanovich, Inc. 1971.

Argyris, Chris, Schön, D. *Theory in Practice.* Jossey-Bass, 1974.

Argyris, Chris. *Knowledge for Action.* Josey-Bass, 1993.

Argyris, Chris. *Overcoming Organizational Defenses.* Allyn and Bacon, 1990.

Autry, James. *Love & Profit.* William Morrow, 1991.

Barrett, F. (1995) Creating Appreciative Learning Cultures. Organizational Dynamics, 24(1), 36-49.

Barrett, F. Cooperrider, D. "Generative Metaphor Intervention: A New Approach for Working with Systems Divided by Conflict and Caught in Defensive Perception." *The Journal of Applied Behavioral Science,* Vol. 26,2. NTL Institute, 1990.

Collins, James, Porras, Jerry. *Built to Last.* HarperBusiness, 1994.

Cooperrider, David, Srivasva, S. "Appreciative Inquiry in Organizational Life" in Woodman, Pasmore (eds.), *Research on Organizational Change and Development,* Vol. 1, JAI Press, 1987.

Cooperrider, David. "Positive Image, Positive Action: The Affirmative Basis of Organizing. *Appreciative Management and Leadership: The Power of Positive Thought and Action in Organizations.* Jossey-Bass, 1990.

EEOC, Spring 1995. Theories of Discrimination. U.S. Government Document.

Ellis, C., Sonnenfeld, J. "Diverse Approaches to Managing Diversity." *Human Resource Management, Spring,* 1994, Vol. 33, Number 1, 79-109.

Fry, R., Pasmore, W., "Strengthening Management Education for Executives" in Srivastva, S. *The Executive Mind.* Jossey-Bass, 1983.

Gergen, Ken. *Realities and Relationships.* Harvard University Press, 1994.

Gergen, Ken. *The Saturated Self.* BasicBooks, 1991.

61.

*R*esources

Hammond, S., Royal, C. (1998) *Lessons From The Field: Applying Appreciative Inquiry.* Thin Book Publishing Co. Out of print.

Johnson, P., Cooperrider, DL. "Finding a Path with Heart: Global Social Change Organizations and their Challenge for the Field of Organizational Development.", in Woodman, Pasmore (eds.), *Research on Organizational Change and Development,* Vol. 5, JAI Press, 1991.

Jung, C. *Modern Man in Search of a Soul.* New York: Harcourt, Brace & Company, 1933.

Mink, O.G., Mink, B.P, and Owen, K.Q. *Groups at Work.* Englewood Cliffs, NJ.: Educational Technology Publications, 1987.

Mohrman, A., Mohrman, S, Ledford, G., Cummings, T., Lawler, E. *Large-Scale Organizational Change.* Jossey-Bass, 1989.

Schein, Edgar. *Organizational Culture and Leadership.* Jossey-Bass, 1992.

Senge, Peter. *The Fifth Disciple.* Doubleday, 1990.

Srivastva, S. Fry, R,. *Executive and Organizational Continuity.* Jossey-Bass, 1992.

Srivastva, Suresh, Cooperrider, David. *Appreciative Management and Leadership: The Power of Positive Thought and Action in Organizations.* Jossey-Bass, 1990.

Weick, K. *Sensemaking in Organizations.* Sage Publications, 1995.

White, T.H. Working in Interesting Times. *Vital Speeches of the Day.* May 15, 1996. Vol. LXII, No.15.

Weisbord, Marvin. *Discovering Common Ground.* Berrett-Koehler Publishers, 1992.

Whyte, David. *The Heart Aroused: Poetry & the Preservation of the Soul in Corporate America.* Doubleday Currency.

Reitman, V. Cramming for the Exotic U.S. Workplace. *The Wall Street Journal.* 7/9/96.

Watkins, J.M., Mohr, B.J. *Appreciative Inquiry.* Jossey-Bass, 2001.

Personal Coaching Sessions

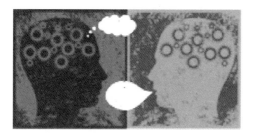

Now offering **Personal Coaching Sessions For Leaders** with Sue Hammond, to review two essential leadership skills: **listening & team leadership**.

Sue will debrief your Inscape Publishing Personal Listening or Team Dimensions Profile with you. She will show you how to use your strengths and adjust your style as needed.

- Individual, 30 minute session

- Uses Inscape Publishing Personal Listening or Team Dimensions Profiles

Order Now! at www.thinbook.com or 888.316.9544

Thin Book iPhone Apps

iPhone Apps – based on your favorite Thin Books:

- **Smart Coach**
- **Trust Tips**
- **TrustTalk**
- **SOAR**
- And more to come...

**Check them out at
www.thinbook.com**

Thin Book eBooks

All Thin Books are now available as ebooks that can be read on you favorite ebook reader, including:

- Kindle
- iPad
- Nook
- Sony Reader

**Check them out at
www.thinbook.com**